Animals That SLITHER AND SLIDE

SLITHERING SNAKES

Enslow PUBLISHING

BY THERESA EMMINIZER

Please visit our website, www.enslow.com. For a free color catalog of all our high-quality books, call toll free 1-800-398-2504 or fax 1-877-980-4454.

Library of Congress Cataloging-in-Publication Data

Names: Emminizer, Theresa, author.
Title: Slithering snakes / Theresa Emminizer.
Description: Buffalo : Enslow Publishing, [2024] | Series: Animals that
   slither and slide | Includes index.
Identifiers: LCCN 2023034787 (print) | LCCN 2023034788 (ebook) | ISBN
   9781978537415 (library binding) | ISBN 9781978537408 (paperback) | ISBN
   9781978537422 (ebook)
Subjects: LCSH: Snakes–Juvenile literature.
Classification: LCC QL666.O6 E46 2024 (print) | LCC QL666.O6 (ebook) |
   DDC 597.96–dc23/eng/20230811
LC record available at https://lccn.loc.gov/2023034787
LC ebook record available at https://lccn.loc.gov/2023034788

Published in 2024 by
Enslow Publishing
2544 Clinton Street
Buffalo, NY 14224

Copyright © 2024 Enslow Publishing

Designer: Leslie Taylor
Editor: Theresa Emminizer

Photo credits: Cover (snake) Dwi Yoga Pujo Laksono/Shutterstock.com, (slime background) AMarc/Shutterstock.com, (brush stroke) Sonic_S/Shutterstock.com, (slime frame) klyaksun/Shutterstock.com; Series Art (slime blob) Lemberg Vector studio/Shutterstock.com; p. 5 Tomas Kotouc/Shutterstock.com; p.7 Nikolay Zaborskikh/Shutterstock.com; p.9 Monica Martinez Do-Allo/Shutterstock.com; p.11 Mark_Kostich/Shutterstock.com; p.13 Mark_Kostich/Shutterstock.com; p.15 Patrick K. Campbell/Shutterstock.com; p.17 Chantelle Bosch/Shutterstock.com; p.19 (black mamba) Craig Cordier/Shutterstock.com, (sea snake) NickEvansKZN/Shutterstock.com; p.21 In The Light Photography/Shutterstock.com.

Some of the images in this book illustrate individuals who are models. The depictions do not imply actual situations or events.

Printed in the United States of America

CPSIA compliance information: Batch #CW24ENS: For further information contact Enslow Publishing, at 1-800-398-2504.

Find us on

CONTENTS

Boldface words appear in
Words to Know.

SNEAKY SNAKES

Eek! It's a snake! Snakes are long, smooth, **slithery** animals without legs. They can be found all over the world. There are more than 3,000 species, or kinds, of snakes. Most live on land, but some live in oceans.

Snakes that live in the ocean are called sea snakes.

5

SNAKE EYES

Have you seen a snake's creepy stare? Snakes don't blink! That's because they don't have moveable eyelids. Some snakes have special body parts called pits close to their eyes. These pits are holes that sense heat, helping a snake find **prey** even when they can't see it.

6

PIT

Rattlesnakes use pits near their eyes to sense heat when hunting prey.

7

A FORKED TONGUE

Snakes have long tongues. The tongues are forked, which means they have two tips. The tips of a snake's tongue are called tines. Snakes use tines to smell! They **flick** their tongues to stir up the air and pick up **particles** to smell.

Having two tines on their tongue helps snakes know where a smell is coming from.

9

A SNAKE'S SKIN

A snake's skin doesn't grow with it. Instead, as snakes get bigger, they grow new skin. Then they shed, or take off, their old skin! Young snakes shed their skin every couple of weeks. Older snakes shed their skin four to six times a year.

If you find a snake's skin, never pick it up with your bare hands! It can make you sick.

11

FIERCE FANGS

Some snakes are **venomous**. They have fangs, or long, sharp teeth, that are **hollow**. When the snake bites, the venom goes into their prey. There are different kinds of snake venom. Some are very deadly, others less so.

This bush viper snake is venomous.

13

SNAKY SLITHERS

Different snake species move in different ways. Some slither in a wavy S shape. This helps them push past rocks or other things in their way. Other snakes move up and down like a caterpillar. This is a useful movement for large snakes.

The green anaconda is a larger snake that uses caterpillar movement.

15

SIDEWINDING AND FLYING

Some snakes are sidewinders. They lift their body in a wave-like movement. Sidewinding is useful for snakes who live in sandy places. Some snakes that live in trees can glide, or move through the air. It's almost like they're flying!

16

Sidewinders lift their bodies over hot sand.

17

SLITHER SPEED

What snakes move the fastest? The African black mamba can reach speeds of 12 miles (19 km) per hour. The yellow-bellied sea snake swims for short periods at 3.3 feet (1 m) per second.

18

BLACK MAMBA

YELLOW-BELLIED
SEA SNAKE

19

SCARY OR SPECIAL?

Snakes might look a little scary, but their interesting **adaptations** make them special animals! Their bodies and **behavior** help them survive, or live, in all sorts of different places. What do you think about slithery snakes? Are they creepy or cute?

20

Some people keep snakes as pets! But remember, never touch a snake in the wild.

21

WORDS TO KNOW

adaptation: A change of an animal or plant that makes it better able to live in certain conditions or a certain place.

behavior: The way an animal acts.

flick: To use with a quick movement.

hollow: Having a hole or empty space inside.

particle: A very small piece of something.

prey: An animal that is hunted by other animals for food.

slithery: Having a surface, texture, or quality that is slippery.

venomous: Able to produce a liquid called venom that is harmful to other animals.

FOR MORE INFORMATION

BOOKS

Hand, Carol. *Snakes*. Minneapolis, MN: Abdo Reference, 2023.

Hughes, Sloane. *20 Things You Didn't Know About Reptile Adaptations*. New York, NY: Rosen Publishing, 2023.

WEBSITES

Humane Wildlife Control Society
wildlifehumane.org/animals/snakes/snake-skin
Learn what to do if you find a snake's skin.

National Geographic Kids
kids.nationalgeographic.com/nature/article/super-snakes
Learn more about snakes and their special adaptations!

INDEX